KT-548-210

The
Battle of
Hastings

14 October 1066

KINGSTON LIBRARIES
KT 0780078 1
WITHDRAWN

The
Battle of
Hastings

14 October 1066

CHERRYTREE BOOKS

A Cherrytree Book

This edition published in 2007
by Cherrytree Books, part of
The Evans Publishing Group
2A Portman Mansions
Chiltern Street
London WIU 6NR

All rights reserved. No part of this publication may be
reproduced, stored in a retrieval system, or transmitted, in
any form, or by any means, electronic, mechanical,
photocopying or otherwise, without prior permission of the
Evans Publishing Group.

British Library Cataloguing in Publication Data

Malam, John
    The Battle of Hastings. – (Dates with history)
    I. Hastings, Battle of England, 1066 – Juvenile literature
    I. Title
    942'. 021

ISBN 182342916
13 digit ISBN 9781842344040

© Evans Publishing Group 2005

Printed in China by WKT Co. Ltd.

KINGSTON UPON THAMES Libraries	
1016070 1	
J942.021	PETERS
06-Aug-2010	£5.99
TD	

Picture credits:
The art archive: 15, 20, 21, 26
The Bridgeman Art Library (with special authorisation of the
    city of Bayeux): 7, 10, 11, 14, 18, 23, 24, 25, 27, 29, 31
Corbis: 19
Istockphoto: front cover
Mary Evans Picture Library: 13, 16, 17
With thanks to the West Stow Anglo-Saxon Village for the
    use of their image on p.8.

To contact the author, please visit his website:
www.johnmalam.co.uk

Contents

A momentous year

The year 1066 was a turning point in English history. That year, a bright light with a long, fiery tail was seen moving across the night sky. It was a comet – a ball of dust, ice and gas – but at the time no one would have known what a comet was. To many people, it seemed as though fire was raining down from the heavens, and they were afraid. They believed the comet was a bad **omen** – a sign of trouble ahead. And they were right.

This map locates the key towns and battlefields of 1066.

Within the space of twelve months, England witnessed the death of two English kings, was **invaded** by two foreign armies and fought three major battles. The final battle was the Battle of Hastings, at which the English were defeated.

The foreign invaders were **Viking**s from Norway, and **Norman**s from Normandy (a region in northern France). The leader of the Norman army was William, Duke of

Normandy. Soon after his army defeated the English at Hastings, he was crowned King William I of England. In the years that followed, he gained control of all England and became known as 'William the **Conqueror**'.

About fifteen years after the Battle of Hastings, English nuns in Canterbury were asked to make an embroidery for the cathedral at Bayeux, a town in Normandy. Using eight colours of wool, they stitched a series of pictures and words on to a strip of linen 70 metres long and 50 centimetres wide. Their embroidery, which is known as the **Bayeux Tapestry**, tells the story of England's conquest at the hands of the Normans.

To this day, English people remember 1066 as the last time an army invaded and conquered England. It was a momentous year.

A panel from the Bayeux Tapestry. The comet which appeared in the sky in 1066 can be seen at the top of the panel.

Anglo-Saxon England in 1066

In the years preceding the Norman conquest, England was largely under **Anglo-Saxon** rule. Starting in the 400s AD, Saxons, Angles and Jutes had come to Britain from northern Europe. Collectively, they have become known as Anglo-Saxons. They settled in the southern part of Britain and named it 'England'. The Anglo-Saxons were the first people to be called 'English'. They spoke a language that was the ancestor of the modern English language.

Anglo-Saxon England grew into a wealthy country. By the year 955 AD, the three separate kingdoms of **Wessex**, **Northumbria** and **Mercia** had become united into one

A reconstruction of a traditional Saxon house at West Stow Anglo-Saxon Village, Suffolk.

country, under the rule of one king. The country was divided into shires, each of which had a main town and a court of law. The shires were sub-divided into smaller areas called 'hundreds', each of which originally contained one hundred households.

By 1066, about one and a half million people lived in England, scattered among some 13,500 villages and towns. London had a population of about 25,000 and was England's largest town. Winchester and York, though smaller, were also important towns. But the countryside was where the majority of people lived, earning their living from the land, particularly from sheep farming.

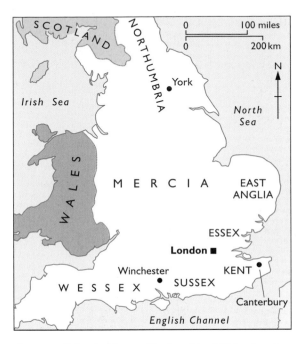

A map of Anglo-Saxon England in 1066, showing the old Saxon kingdoms and principal towns.

People in Anglo-Saxon England enjoyed comparative peace and prosperity in the years leading up to the Battle of Hastings. But the threat of invasion, particularly from the Vikings, was never far away. Moreover, King Edward the **Confessor's** weak leadership had encouraged rivalry between the powerful **earls** who still controlled the lands of Wessex, Northumbria and Mercia.

Edward, King of England

The Battle of Hastings of 1066 was the final act in a vital power struggle. It was a fight between two rival leaders to decide which of them would become the next king of England.

The story begins many years before the battle, during the reign of King Edward the Confessor. Although Edward was born in England, his mother was a Norman, and he was brought up in Normandy. He had many friends who were high-ranking Normans, and was strongly influenced by them.

An illuminated manuscript showing King Edward the Confessor at his coronation in 1042.

Edward returned to England in 1041, and was crowned king the following year. Edward had always been deeply religious, and as his **reign** progressed his religious zeal grew. He spent much of his time praying and confessing his sins to God. To his people, Edward seemed more like a monk than a king, and for this he came to be known as 'Edward the Confessor'. One of his greatest achievements was the building of Westminster Abbey in London. It was built to look like a Norman cathedral.

Westminster Abbey in the 18th century. Its construction was begun in about 1050 and it still stands in London today.

King Edward died on 5 January 1066 and was buried in his new abbey at Westminster. Who should succeed him as the next king of England? It was not an easy question to answer. Edward had never had children, which meant there was no one in the royal family to inherit his crown, and a distant relative – a 14-year-old prince called Edgar – was judged to be too young to be king. England's crown would have to pass to whoever had the strongest claim to it.

Rivals for the English crown

After King Edward's death in 1066, three men stepped forward to lay claim to the throne of England.

An illustration of Duke William of Normandy, one of the three rivals for the English crown in 1066.

One of the three rivals for the English crown was Harold Sigurdsson, a Viking. He was the king of Norway and was nicknamed Harold Hardrada, meaning 'Harold the Stern'. He claimed the crown of England had been promised to his father by King Harthacnut, who had been England's king immediately before King Edward. Harold Hardrada wanted this promise to be kept. Under Harold Hardrada, England would be ruled by a Norwegian king.

The second contender for the English throne was William, Duke of Normandy. William claimed that King Edward, who was his second cousin, had promised him the English throne in 1051. Edward may have made this promise as a way of thanking the Normans for the protection they had given him when he lived in Normandy. Under William, England would be ruled by a Norman king.

The third man to claim the right to be the next king of England was Harold Godwinson, the Earl of Wessex and a member of a leading Anglo-Saxon family. Harold's sister, Edith, had married King Edward, and this made Harold and Edward brothers-in-law. Harold was the most powerful man in England after the king. He was a soldier and commanded the king's army.

Harold Godwinson, Earl of Wessex and brother-in-law to King Edward the Confessor.

As King Edward lay dying, he named Harold as his successor to the English throne. By doing this, Edward broke his promise to Duke William. He may have done so to please the English nobles, since Edward knew they wanted England to be ruled by an Englishman.

The road to invasion

On the day after Edward's death, Harold Godwinson was crowned King Harold II of England. The news soon reached Duke William in Normandy. He was furious and believed that he had been utterly betrayed. Not only had King Edward broken his promise to him, but, according to Norman accounts written years later, Harold had also double-crossed him.

The Norman version of the story claims that, in 1064, Harold was shipwrecked off the coast of Normandy. He was rescued by a French nobleman, who then took Harold prisoner. William is said to have arranged for Harold's release, in exchange for his promise that William would become the next king of England on Edward's

The Bayeux Tapestry shows Harold touching two holy relics as he promises that Duke William will be England's next king.

death. In William's eyes, Harold's actions made him a thief and a liar and he vowed to oppose him. In the spring of 1066, William ordered ships to be built to transport his army to England. By the end of the summer, he had assembled a powerful invasion force of about 750 vessels. He had also won the blessing of Pope Alexander II for his mission.

Pope Alexander II (second from left) supported William's invasion of England, even giving him a banner to carry into battle.

Harold had another dangerous enemy in his brother, Tostig, the Earl of Northumbria. In 1065, there was a uprising in Northumbria and Tostig asked Harold to help him defeat the rebels. Harold refused, and Tostig was forced to flee from his lands. Thereafter, Tostig turned against his brother, blaming him for his downfall.

Within weeks of becoming king, Harold realised that England faced imminent invasion by two armies. The north of the country was threatened by Harold Hardrada invading from Norway; the south by the Normans, headed by Duke William.

King Harold Hardrada invades England

The first sign of real trouble for Harold came from his brother, Tostig. In May 1066, Tostig's ships raided the south coast of England before sailing north to Scotland. In Scotland, Tostig made a pact with Harold Hardrada, King of Norway, whereby he agreed to support Hardrada in his invasion of England.

Harold Hardrada and his men crossed the North Sea to England in traditional Viking warships like this one.

In early September 1066, Hardrada set sail from Norway with 500 ships. As he approached the English coast, his fleet was joined by Tostig's ships and they sailed together along the River Ouse towards the city of York. They marched on the city with a force of 5,000 men. At Fulford Gate, just outside York, they were met by an English army of equal size. In the battle that followed, the English were defeated and Hardrada and Tostig captured York. Rather than occupy the city itself, the invaders camped outside it, at Stamford Bridge.

This picture, from the 19th century, shows King Harold defeating Harold Hardrada at the Battle of Stamford Bridge in 1066.

News of Hardrada's victory soon reached King Harold. He suddenly had a crucial decision to make: should he travel north to face Hardrada, or remain in the south to confront Duke William when he invaded? Harold decided to attack Hardrada. With an army of 6,000 men on horseback, he covered the 400 kilometres from London to York in just four days.

Hardrada and Tostig did not expect Harold and his men to move so fast, and were taken by surprise. On 25 September, five days after the Battle of Fulford Gate, the second key battle of 1066 took place – the Battle of Stamford Bridge. It was a convincing victory for the new English king, and both Hardrada and Tostig were killed in the bloody battle.

Duke William invades England

The north wind played an important role in the events of 1066. It had blown Hardrada's ships towards England – but while the wind helped him, it stalled William's invasion. As long as the wind blew from the north, William's ships could not leave their harbour, for they risked being blown straight back to Normandy.

Two days after the Battle of Stamford Bridge, the wind began to blow from the south and the Norman ships were made ready to sail the 90 kilometres to England.

A panel from the Bayeux Tapestry, showing Duke William and the Norman fleet sailing across the English Channel.

At the head of the fleet was William, in his ship the *Mora*. On the morning of 28 September, William's army of 7,500 men landed at Pevensey, Sussex. There was no attempt made to prevent them from landing.

According to a story written some years later, William tripped as he stepped ashore. This could have been seen as a bad omen. Instead, as he fell to the ground, he is said to have grabbed a handful of soil. This was believed to be a sign that he had England in his grasp.

The remains of Pevensey Castle, Sussex. Duke William and the Norman army landed on the coast close to the ancient castle.

The Norman army marched east along the coast to Hastings, where they set up camp. Over the next few days, the army built a wooden fort and began to **devastate** the surrounding area, burning villages and seizing food and supplies. William's plan was to lure Harold towards him. He was setting a trap for the English king.

King Harold goes to Hastings

Harold was still in the north of England when William's fleet landed on the south coast. As soon as he heard the news, Harold gathered what remained of his weary troops and marched back to London. From there, he sent a monk to William with the message that King Edward had named Harold as his successor, and that he was therefore the rightful king of England, not William. Duke William responded by sending one of his own monks to Harold, with a message that rejected Harold's claim to the crown outright. After this there would be no more **diplomacy**. Only a battle would decide which man should rule England.

The Norman troops lead their horses on to English soil in this scene from the Bayeux Tapestry.

Taking what troops he could **muster** in London, Harold set out for the town of Hastings, 90 kilometres to the south. On the way more men joined his army, swelling the numbers to about 8,000 troops – fewer than Harold would have liked, but still slightly larger than William's army. Harold's intention may have been to cut William off at Hastings, keeping him inside the town and stopping supplies from getting through to him. A **siege** could have starved William and his army into surrender. Another possibility is that Harold planned to mount a surprise attack on William, as he had done with Harold Hardrada at Stamford Bridge.

In the event, Harold used neither of these tactics. William's scouts spotted Harold's army as it approached Hastings and the element of surprise was lost. William's soldiers took up their positions, ready for battle.

A Norman sentry warns Duke William (far left) of the English army's approach.

The Battle of Hastings

At about 9 o'clock on the morning of Saturday 14 October 1066, trumpets sounded and the Battle of Hastings began. Harold's army was in position along a ridge about 11 kilometres from Hastings. The English called the ridge Santlache ('Sandy Stream'), but later it was given a Norman name – Senlac, which was French for 'Blood Lake'. Harold's troops were crowded together on the ridge, but were in the better tactical position as the Normans were forced to attack uphill.

William attacked first. His **archers** fired waves of arrows towards Harold's men, who held their long shields close together to form a **'shield-wall'**. Many arrows fell short,

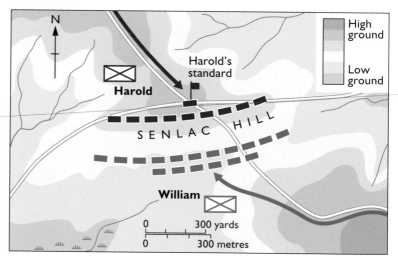

The positions of the English and Norman camps and armies at the beginning of the Battle of Hastings.

others stuck into the English shields. The arrow attack lasted a few minutes, then faded away as the Norman archers ran out of ammunition. Harold's troops stood firm on the ridge.

William then ordered his foot-soldiers to charge up the hill. As they did, they were struck down by English arrows, spears and **slingstones**. But many Normans survived the barrage of missiles thrown at them and soon they were upon the English, fighting hand-to-hand with swords. It was an evenly balanced fight, and when William realised that his troops were not gaining any ground, he sent in his **cavalry** in support of the foot-soldiers. The men on horseback charged bravely up the slope of the hill, but they too were fought back by King Harold's troops.

The Norman cavalry, clutching their spears, charge uphill towards the English army.

By midday the Norman army was tiring. Suddenly, the cavalry and foot-soldiers fled back down the hill, chased by English soldiers. Then a wild rumour spread among the troops that William had been killed in battle. It was a dangerous moment for the invaders, when panic could easily have set in.

Duke William (centre) raises his helmet to show his men that he is still alive.

Instead, what happened next proved to be a turning point in the battle. William raised his helmet and showed his face to his troops. When they saw he was alive they rallied again, and William led his cavalry against the English soldiers who had broken away from the safety of their shield-wall. They were cut down where they stood.

By early afternoon both sides had lost many men, but King Harold's army still stood firm on the summit of the ridge. William realised that to win the battle he had to find a way of breaking through the English shield-wall. Remembering how the English had earlier broken rank to chase his men down the hill, he ordered his cavalry to charge, then turn and flee. It was a clever tactic, and it worked. Believing the Normans were retreating, English soldiers chased after them – only to find, to their horror, that they had been tricked, as the Norman cavalry turned and struck them down. Norman archers then showered arrows on to the ridge, breaking holes in the English line. The battle was turning in William's favour.

At some point in the afternoon, King Harold was killed. According to a famous scene in the Bayeux Tapestry, Harold was wounded by an arrow that hit him in the eye. As he fell back, a Norman warrior on horseback hacked at him with his sword. Above the pictures are the Latin words for 'King Harold has been killed'.

King Harold is struck in the eye by an arrow (left), then hacked to the ground by a Norman soldier (right).

The Norman Conquest of England

The death of Harold was a great shock to his men, from which they never recovered. It had the opposite effect on the Normans, who continued to fight until they reached the top of the ridge, causing the English to scatter and flee. The victory was William's.

Some time later, Harold's body was identified on the battlefield and taken away for burial at Waltham Abbey, Essex. Harold Godwinson, the last Anglo-Saxon king of England, had been king for just forty weeks.

Battle Abbey was built on the orders of William the Conqueror on the site where King Harold was killed.

William had defeated Harold, but that alone did not make him king of England. He now had to win the support of England's earls and church leaders. Some nobles proclaimed 14-year-old Prince Edgar (see page 11) to be the new king, but he was never crowned.

After resting for a few days at Hastings, William and his army marched to London. They dealt brutally with any resistance they encountered on the way, slaughtering rebels and burning whole villages. In London, William was met by the Archbishop of York, the boy-king Edgar and leading earls. They swore an **oath** of loyalty to William, and offered him the crown. On Christmas Day 1066, Duke William was crowned King William I of England at Westminster Abbey.

The crowning of King William I of England, 25 December 1066.

William was England's first Norman king. Although he had gained the crown by force, he wanted the English to think of him as their rightful king, as chosen by Edward the Confessor. Over the next few years, King William defeated rebellions in many parts of England and when the country was at peace, the famous Norman Conquest was complete. The Norman duke who had become king of England was known thereafter as 'William the Conqueror'.

Timeline

1042	*8 June:* Edward the Confessor becomes king of England.
1050	The construction of Westminster Abbey, London, begins.
1051	King Edward is believed to have promised William, Duke of Normandy, the crown of England.
1053	*15 April:* Harold Godwinson becomes the Earl of Wessex.
1055	Harold Godwinson's brother, Tostig, becomes the Earl of Northumbria.
1064	Harold Godwinson is said to have sworn an oath offering his support to William in his claim to the crown of England.
1066	*5 January:* King Edward dies.
1066	*6 January:* King Edward is buried in Westminster Abbey. Harold Godwinson is crowned King Harold II of England at St Paul's Cathedral, London.
1066	*24 April*: A comet (now known as Halley's Comet) becomes visible in the sky.
1066	*early September:* King Harold Hardrada and his Norwegian army invade northern England.
1066	*20 September:* Battle of Fulford Gate, near York. King Harold Hardrada and Earl Tostig defeat an English army.
1066	*20-24 September:* King Harold marches his army north.

1066	*25 September:* Battle of Stamford Bridge, near York. King Harold defeats the Norwegian army. Harold Hardrada and Earl Tostig are killed.
1066	*28 September:* William, Duke of Normandy, lands on the south coast of England at Pevensey, Sussex.
1066	*1 October:* King Harold learns that William has invaded. He and his men set off from Stamford Bridge to face the Normans.
1066	*14 October:* Battle of Hastings, Sussex. William defeats King Harold of England. Harold is killed during the battle.
1066	*25 December:* William is crowned King William I of England in Westminster Abbey.
1077–87	The Bayeux Tapestry is made, probably at Canterbury, Kent.
1087	*9 September:* William the Conqueror dies. His third son is crowned William II of England.

Glossary

Anglo-Saxon The name for the inhabitants of England between about 500 and 1100 AD.

archers Soldiers who fire arrows.

Bayeux Tapestry A long, embroidered cloth decorated with words and pictures that tell the story of the Battle of Hastings.

cavalry Soldiers who fight on horseback.

confess To admit to doing wrong. Confessing is an important part of the Catholic religion.

conquer To defeat and take control of a place.

devastate To destroy something.

diplomacy Using peaceful means to prevent a conflict.

earls English nobles.

invade To enter and occupy a place by force.

Mercia Saxon kingdom in central England.

muster To bring a group of people together.

Norman People from Normandy, a region of northern France.

Northumbria A Saxon kingdom in the north of England.

oath A solemn promise.

omen An event taken to show what will happen in the future.

reign The length of time a king or queen rules.

relic Something that has survived from the past.

shield-wall When shields are held close together to form a wall.

siege When an army traps an enemy inside a fort or town.

slingstones Stones fired from slings and catapults.

Viking A name for the inhabitants of Scandinavia, between about 800 and 1100 AD.

Wessex A Saxon kingdom in the south of England.

Who's Who?

Alexander II (died 1073) Pope from 1061. Gave his blessing to William's invasion of England.

Edgar (c.1052–c.1125) 14-year-old English prince chosen as king after the death of King Harold. King of England from October to December, 1066.

Edward (c.1005–1066) King of England from 1042. Known as 'Edward the Confessor'. Promised the English crown to Duke William of Normandy, and also to Harold Godwinson.

Harold II (Harold Godwinson, c.1016–1066) King of England from January to October 1066. The last Saxon king. Killed in the Battle of Hastings.

Harold Sigurdsson (died 1066) King of Norway from 1046. The last Viking invader of England. Known as 'Harold Hardrada'. Killed in the Battle of Stamford Bridge.

Harthacnut (c.1019–1042) King of England from 1040. Half-brother to Edward the Confessor.

Tostig (c.1025–1066) Earl of Northumbria, brother of King Harold. Killed in the Battle of Stamford Bridge.

William I (1027–1087) Duke of Normandy from 1035, king of England from 1066. Known as 'William the Conqueror'.

A silver coin depicting the head of King William I of England.

Index